Books available by Brendan Kennelly

FEDERICO GARCÍA LORCA

BLOOD WEDDING

(Bodas de Sangre)

A NEW VERSION BY
BRENDAN KENNELLY

BLOODAXE BOOKS

First published 1996 by
Bloodaxe Books Ltd,
P.O. Box 1SN,
Newcastle upon Tyne NE99 1SN.

Bloodaxe Books Ltd acknowledges
the financial assistance of Northern Arts.

Cover printing by J. Thomson Colour Printers Ltd, Glasgow.

Printed in Great Britain by
Bell & Bain Limited, Glasgow, Scotland.

BLOOD WEDDING

Brendan Kennelly's new version of *Blood Wedding* by Federico García Lorca was first performed by Northern Stage at Newcastle Playhouse on 23 October 1996. This production was staged in Newcastle from 23 October to 2 November and at Derby Playhouse from 6 to 23 November 1996. The cast (in order of Lorca's text) at the first performance was as follows:

MOTHER *of bridegroom*	Alison Peebles
BRIDE	Melanie MacHugh
MOTHER-IN-LAW *of Leonardo*	Charo Peinado
WIFE *of Leonardo*	Esperanza Gil
SERVANT, *maid to bride*	Carol McGuigan
NEIGHBOUR *of bridegroom's mother*	Sarah Kemp
GIRLS	Andrea Puerta
	Clare Mann
LEONARDO	Alec Westwood
BRIDEGROOM	Ciaran McMahon
FATHER *of bride*	John Cobb
THE MOON	Richard Clews
DEATH *(as a beggar woman)*	Sarah Kemp
WOODCUTTERS	Francisco Alfonsin
	John Cobb
	Mañuel Canadas
SINGER	Maureen Jelks

(All other parts played by members of the company.)

ARTISTIC DIRECTOR	Alan Lyddiard
DESIGNER	Neil Murray
LIGHTING DESIGNER	Tina MacHugh
MUSICAL COMPOSER & DIRECTOR	Alistair Anderson
CHOREOGRAPHER	Salud Lopez
MUSICIANS	Alistair Anderson
	Clare Mann
COMPANY STAGE MANAGER	Amanda Purvis
FIRST ASSISTANT DIRECTOR	Samantha Kelly (ACE trainee)
SECOND ASSISTANT DIRECTOR	Richard Beecham
DEPUTY STAGE MANAGER	Colin Sutherland
ASSISTANT STAGE MANAGERS	Steven Allen
	Ruth Moore

Northern Stage at Newcastle Playhouse is funded by: Arts Council of England, Northern Arts, City of Newcastle upon Tyne, University of Newcastle. *Blood Wedding* received a special mention from the Council of Europe and support from CrossCountry.

NOTE

In trying to unearth a fit English for Lorca's *Blood Wedding* I found, or found myself believing, that there is a dynamic equation at work: for Lorca, sex in life is the equivalent of poetry in drama. It is a vitalising, dangerous ever-presence. It is essential and pervasive; it can be inspiringly unifying or tragically divisive. To live with that knowledge and to write out of that conviction is to explore the limits of poetic and dramatic daring. Lorca is instinctively daring. For him, poetry is linguistic, imagistic, rhythmical and emotional revolution. *Blood Wedding* is a play about sexual and poetic/dramatic daring in which the poetry of violence is one with the violence of poetry. In this climate of sustained daring, the moon's cosmic longing and death's insatiable lust stress the passionate revolution and hungry quest of the blood-lovers; the moon and death are a completely natural, licentious chorus as well as a chilling, elemental pair of lovers in their own trans-human light and darkness. Lorca's daring knows no bounds; his imagination riots and orders among forces that are real, troubling and forbidden by ourselves to ourselves. He lives in, and stubbornly explores, those areas that made the recurring 'Thou shalt not' of the Commandments towering and necessary injunctions, as necessary and towering, indeed, as the impulse to rebel against the ethical tyranny of that very same 'Thou shalt not'.

Longing spawns and nurtures Lorca's spirit of daring. *Blood Wedding* is shot through with fierce longing of different kinds; yet each kind has a sexual radiance, the varying intensity of which is at once regional and local as well as cosmic and universal: a demented horse-rider shares with the articulate moon an undeniable longing for love. All the resources of Lorca's audacity as a poetic dramatist are brought to bear on this drama where human passion is explored with the same penetration as the phenomenon of lunar longing and function. It is precisely this incisive adventurousness that prompts a translator, or version-maker (a term I prefer), to draw on *connections* within the play that have the most startling and revealing effects on his/her efforts to comprehend it as a coherent dramatic work. I only hope that this version of Lorca's explosive, exploratory masterpiece captures something of this poet's fearless spirit.

BRENDAN KENNELLY

ACT ONE

SCENE ONE

Yellow room.

BRIDEGROOM. (*Coming in.*) Mother.

MOTHER. Yes?

BRIDEGROOM. I'm going.

MOTHER. Where?

BRIDEGROOM. The vineyard. (*Starts to go.*)

MOTHER. Hold on a moment.

BRIDEGROOM. Yes?

MOTHER. Your breakfast.

BRIDEGROOM. Forget it. I'll have grapes. Where's the knife?

MOTHER. The knife? What for?

BRIDEGROOM. (*Laughing.*) To cut them.

MOTHER. (*Muttering.*) The knife, the knife...The curse of God on all the knives and the devil's knacker that invented them.

BRIDEGROOM. Forget it.

MOTHER. And the curse of God on guns, machine guns, rifles, pistols...and knives, even the smallest knife...and scythes and pitchforks.

BRIDEGROOM. All right.

MOTHER. The curse of God on anything that can cut and hack and rip the body of a man, a beautiful man in the prime of his life, going out to the vineyards, taking care of his olives, because they are his, his alone, part of his inheritance.

BRIDEGROOM. Mother, be easy.

MOTHER. ...and that beautiful man does not return. Or if he does come back, it's to put rock salt on his body to stop him swelling. How in God's name can you carry a knife on your body? How in God's name can I put up with this serpent in the chest? (*Takes out knife from chest.*)

BRIDEGROOM. Can you speak of nothing else?

11

MOTHER. No, as long as I live I shall speak of nothing else. First, your father. His body smelt of carnations; I knew the pleasure of his body for three brief years. Your brother next. Where's justice? How can a small knife or a small gun finish the life of a fine, handsome bull of a man? Easy? – no, I'll not be easy, I'll never be easy. The days melt and wither and hopelessness claws at my eyes, claws deep into the roots of my hair, steals into my blood, lives there.

BRIDEGROOM. Stop!

MOTHER. I'll never stop! Who'll bring your father back to me? Or your brother? Then there's the jail. What's a jail? The murderers live there, eat there, sleep there, smoke there, play there, make music there. These murderers enjoy sweet music. And the bodies of my two dead men are all dust and worms and obscene weeds...all dust...and silence...two men – like two geraniums – ...and their murderers, bloated in jail, alive and carefree, looking at the mountains.

BRIDEGROOM. Are you telling me to kill them?

MOTHER. No...but I must speak. I must speak because you must go out that door. I hate it that you must carry a knife. Why must you go out to the fields? With all my heart I wish you wouldn't go.

BRIDEGROOM. (*Laughs.*) O mother, mother!

MOTHER. I wish you were a woman. I'd love you to be a woman. Then the two of us could embroider white little woolly dogs.

BRIDEGROOM. (*Puts his arms round her.*) Suppose I took you to the vineyards with me.

MOTHER. And what would an old woman be doing in the vineyards? Would you lay me down under the vine-shoots? Would you stretch me out there?

BRIDEGROOM. (*Takes her in his arms, lifts her high.*) O you old woman, you old old woman, you old old old woman, old as time, old as the earth itself.

MOTHER. Your father used to take me there. There was fierce, good breeding in him, the best of blood. Your grandfather left sons behind him wherever he went, strong sons at every twist and turn of his road. And that's what I love: men to be men, grapes to be grapes, wheat to be wheat.

BRIDEGROOM. And me, mother, what about me?

MOTHER. You?

BRIDEGROOM. Do you want me to say it again?

MOTHER. (*Her expression is grave.*) Oh!

BRIDEGROOM. Is it foolish?

MOTHER. No.

BRIDEGROOM. What'll I do?

MOTHER. It's hard to say. It's all so sudden, you've taken me by surprise. She's a good girl. Isn't she? She's a worker. She makes good bread. She knows how to sew. And yet, when I dare to mention her name, demons batter my head with stones, stick long hot needles into my heart.

BRIDEGROOM. That's foolish.

MOTHER. Worse than foolish. I'll be alone. All alone. You're the only man left to me now and it breaks my heart to see you leaving.

BRIDEGROOM. But you must come and live with us.

MOTHER. I can't do that. I can't abandon your father and your brother. I must go to them bright and early every morning. If I leave now, one of the family of the men who murdered them, one of the accursed Felixes, might die and might be buried next to my family. That must never happen! I'll tear a dead Felix up out of the earth with my own hands and smash the corpse in smithereens against the graveyard wall.

BRIDEGROOM. That old story again!

MOTHER. (*Calms.*) Forgive me. (*She pauses.*) How long do you know her?

BRIDEGROOM. For three years. And now the vineyard is mine.

MOTHER. Three years. There was another man in her life, wasn't there?

BRIDEGROOM. I don't know. What man can ever say he knows the whole story of the woman he marries?

MOTHER. True. I never looked at another man. I looked only at your father, him alone, and when they murdered him I looked

13

at a blank wall. A woman has her man, there's nothing else to say.

BRIDEGROOM. My woman is good. The best.

MOTHER. I don't doubt it. What was her mother like? I wish I'd known her.

BRIDEGROOM. Who cares?

MOTHER. (*Looks directly at him.*) Son.

BRIDEGROOM. Yes.

MOTHER. You're right. When do you want me to go and ask for her?

BRIDEGROOM. Sunday? Next Sunday?

MOTHER. The lovely old brass earrings, I'll give her these. And you must buy for her...

BRIDEGROOM. You know more than I.

MOTHER. You must buy stockings for her, and two, no, three suits for yourself. You are all I have in the world.

BRIDEGROOM. I must go now. And tomorrow I must go and see her.

MOTHER. Yes, tomorrow. Six grandchildren. You must make me happy with six grandchildren, or even more, as many children as your heart desires. Your father was robbed of the chance to give them to me.

BRIDEGROOM. The first child will be for you.

MOTHER. Good. And may the children be girls because my heart's wish is to embroider with patient skill, make perfect lace, and taste sweet deep peace all the days of my life.

BRIDEGROOM. You'll love my woman.

MOTHER. I will, I know I will. (*She moves to kiss him; stops.*) On with you. You're too big for my kisses now. Keep all your kisses for your wife. (*Aside.*) The night she is your wife.

BRIDEGROOM. I'm off.

MOTHER. It's time for you to dig the earth near the mill. It's time you paid attention to that, don't you think?

BRIDEGROOM. Yes, yes.

MOTHER. God be with you, son.

(*The* BRIDEGROOM *leaves. The* MOTHER *stays rooted. A* NEIGHBOUR *enters dressed in dark clothes, wearing a shawl.*)

MOTHER. Good neighbour, look at me. What do you see?

NEIGHBOUR. I see a woman that's strong because she knows where she stands. I had to buy things at the shop so I dropped in to see you. We live a long way from each other.

MOTHER. It's twenty years since I walked to the end of the street. Twenty years. Walking that street would be like walking to the end of the world.

NEIGHBOUR. Healthy and well you're looking.

MOTHER. You really think so?

NEIGHBOUR. That's how things are. Yesterday they brought my neighbour's son home – his two hands cut clean off him by the machine. (*She sits.*)

MOTHER. Is it Raphael?

NEIGHBOUR. Yes, that's him. Ah well! You know I often think of our two sons, yours and mine; they're far better off the way they are, safe from being maimed or crippled. What use is a crippled man?

MOTHER. Hold your tongue. There's no comfort in that kind of talk.

(*They sit, sigh. Pause.*)

NEIGHBOUR. Your son, how is he?

MOTHER. He left a while ago.

NEIGHBOUR. He must have bought the vineyard then.

MOTHER. Yes. He had a bit of good luck.

NEIGHBOUR. He'll get married so.

MOTHER. (*Draws closer to her.*) Listen! Listen!

NEIGHBOUR. (*Entering the conspiracy.*) Yes?

MOTHER. Do you know my son's girl?

NEIGHBOUR. Yes, she's good, a good girl.

MOTHER. Yes, yes, but all the same...

NEIGHBOUR. But all the same no one really knows her. She lives with her father, alone, just the two of them, away out there, miles from anywhere. But she's a good girl, a good girl. She's well used to being alone. She knows all about it. It's good to know about being alone if you're going to be married.

MOTHER. Did you know her mother?

NEIGHBOUR. Yes. She was a fine, handsome woman. She was a strong, patient woman, her face seemed to glow like the face of a saint. But I had no time for her, I didn't like her. She showed no love for her husband...

MOTHER. Isn't it amazing, the way people find things out about other people!

NEIGHBOUR. I'm sorry if I've offended you. But I didn't like her. That's the truth. But no one would say if she was decent or not. She was proud, so proud.

MOTHER. Well, now we know, don't we?

NEIGHBOUR. You asked me, didn't you? I told you.

MOTHER. I wish nobody knew the slightest thing about that girl and her mother. I wish they were like two fierce thistles in the corner of a field; they have no names; and if anyone touches them, their sting is never forgotten. Two nameless, fierce and stinging creatures – that's my dream.

NEIGHBOUR. I understand your dream. Your son is worth his weight in gold. No better gift from God than a strong son.

MOTHER. He's strong all right. As strong as I can make him. I look after him. I hear the girl had another man some time ago.

NEIGHBOUR. Yes, when she was fifteen or so. But he's married two years now. To the girl's cousin, in fact. No one seems to recall the engagement, however.

MOTHER. But you recall it! Why?

NEIGHBOUR. The things you ask me!

MOTHER. Who was that other young man in the life of my son's girl?

NEIGHBOUR. Leonardo.

16

MOTHER. Leonardo who?

NEIGHBOUR. Leonardo Felix.

MOTHER. (*Rising.*) Leonardo Felix!

NEIGHBOUR. What are you thinking? Leonardo is not to blame. He was eight years old when these terrible things happened. Will you blame an eight year-old child? An innocent child?

MOTHER. Felix! Felix! That name! When I hear it, my mouth stinks of muck and filth! (*She spits.*) And I must spit, spit, spit, or that filth and muck will poison all my body and my mind. Felix! Murderers of my men, my blood!

NEIGHBOUR. Be easy, be easy, no.

MOTHER. How can I be easy?

NEIGHBOUR. Spit like a mad cat, if you wish, but don't destroy your son's happiness. Don't say a single word to him. Look at yourself! You're an old woman. So am I. Old women should keep their eyes open and their mouths shut.

MOTHER. I won't say a word.

NEIGHBOUR. (*Kisses her.*) Not a word.

MOTHER. (*Calmly.*) Eyes open. Mouth shut.

NEIGHBOUR. I must go. My family will be back soon from the fields.

MOTHER. Have you ever known a day of such burning heat? Such a day it's been! Such a hot day!

NEIGHBOUR. Yes, the children were worn out and black with the sun taking water to the reapers in the fields. God be with you.

MOTHER. God be with you.

(*The* MOTHER *moves, stops, crosses herself.*)

[CURTAIN]

SCENE TWO

Rose-coloured room. Flowers. Copperware. In the centre, a table with a tablecloth. Leonardo's MOTHER-IN-LAW. *Child in her arms, rocking. Leonardo's* WIFE *is mending stockings.*

MOTHER-IN-LAW. Rock on my breast, my sweet baby,
　　Dream of the big black stallion
　　At the water, at the water,
　　But he won't drink it, he won't drink it.
　　See the water deep and black
　　See the trees all tall and strong,
　　The water trots down to the bridge
　　And it sings a magic song.
　　Listen to the water, dearest child,
　　It is singing of its pain.
　　Who knows the meaning of that song?
　　No man, my heart replies, no man.
　　The big black stallion lifts his head
　　And swishes his majestic tail.

WIFE. (*Very quietly.*) Sleep, carnation, let me think
　　Why the stallion will not drink.

MOTHER-IN-LAW. Sleep, my rose, dream deep in sleep,
　　The stallion now begins to weep.

　　The stallion's hooves are covered in blood
　　The stallion's mane is stiff as ice
　　And a broken silver knife
　　Hides behind the stallion's eyes.

　　They galloped down to the riverside
　　Galloped down where the water flowed
　　And though the water galloped fast
　　It couldn't touch his galloping blood.

WIFE. Sleep, carnation, this long day,
　　The stallion turns his head away.
　　Trembling at the water's brink
　　The stallion stares – but will not drink.

MOTHER-IN-LAW. My perfect rose, escape in sleep.
　　The perfect stallion starts to weep.

WIFE. The stallion won't go near that wet place
Though his thirst is great.
He has galloped murderous miles
And his body is all sweat.

Now the stallion starts to neigh
To the mountains cold and high,
His mouth is hot, his throat is parched
And the river is gone dry.

The troubled stallion stands alone.
He will not drink, O pitiful sight,
His pain is like a wicked knife
Stabbing the heart of the morning light.

MOTHER-IN-LAW. Stay away, keep clear, don't touch this house,
Close the window, lock the door,
Steal a dream from the whispering trees,
Cherish that dream for evermore.

WIFE. At last my darling's fast asleep.

MOTHER-IN-LAW. May that sleep be sweet and deep.

WIFE. Stallion, let me tell you this:
My baby's sleep is happiness.

MOTHER-IN-LAW. In a cradle of steel.

WIFE. Baby's quilt is soft and warm.

MOTHER-IN-LAW. In sleep's deep water sweetly sink.

WIFE. The stallion stares at water still
And still he will not drink.

MOTHER-IN-LAW. Stay away, keep clear, don't touch this house,
Close the window, lock the door.
Gallop towards the distant mountain
There you'll find your mare
Waiting in the deep dark valley.
It's time for you to gallop there.

WIFE. Now my child is fast asleep.

MOTHER-IN-LAW. May that sleep be sweet and deep.

WIFE. (*Very quiet.*) My little flower, sweet be your sleep.
Now let the world's shadows creep

About you; you are safe today.
The stallion lowers his head, then turns away.
He will not drink. What can I say?

MOTHER-IN-LAW. (*Quiet.*) Peace to your sleep, my perfect rose.
What do the valley and the mountain know?
Behind his eyes a long knife hides.
The stallion's tears begin to flow.
The water laughs at the stallion's eyes.
In sleep I hear his cries, his cries...

(*She takes away the child.* LEONARDO *comes in.*)

LEONARDO. Where is he?

WIFE. Asleep.

LEONARDO. He was crying in his sleep last night.

WIFE. But he's like a dahlia now.
How are you? Were you at the blacksmith's?

LEONARDO. Yes, I've just come from there. It's amazing! It takes two months to shoe that horse and they fall off him in no time at all. Must be the stones. The stones are cruel.

WIFE. Maybe you ride him too much?

LEONARDO. No. Not all that much.

WIFE. Yesterday a couple of neighbours told me they saw you at the far side of the plains.

LEONARDO. The far side of the plains? Who told you that?

WIFE. The women who gather capers. I was surprised by the news. Was it you?

LEONARDO. It wasn't me. Why in God's name would I go there, over there to that dry wasteland?

WIFE. I thought as much. I said as much. But the horse was fit to drop with exhaustion. The sweat was streaming from him.

LEONARDO. Did you see the horse?

WIFE. No. My mother saw him.

LEONARDO. Is she with the child?

WIFE. She is. Would you like a drink of cold lemon?

LEONARDO. With very good ice-cold water?

WIFE. Why didn't you come home to eat?

LEONARDO. The wheat-weighers kept me. They always manage to
delay me with their talk and stories of what's going on.

WIFE. (*Making lemon drink and very tenderly.*) Did they give you
a good price?

LEONARDO. A fair one.

WIFE. I must get a new dress; and a cap with ribbons for the child.

LEONARDO. (*Gets up.*) I'll go and see him.

WIFE. He's sleeping. Be careful.

MOTHER-IN-LAW. (*Entering.*) Well, who's been racing the horse?
He's worn out. He's lying there, stretched out to God and
the world, the eyes bulging out of him as if some madman
had ridden him without mercy from the other end of the earth.

LEONARDO. (*Sharply.*) I rode him.

MOTHER-IN-LAW. Well, he's your horse, of course.

WIFE. (*Timidly.*) Leonardo was delayed by the wheat-weighers.

MOTHER-IN-LAW. He can drop dead for all I care.

WIFE. Is the drink all right? Is it cold enough?

LEONARDO. Fine.

WIFE. Do you know they're coming to ask for my cousin?

LEONARDO. When?

WIFE. Tomorrow. The wedding will be within a month. We'll be
invited, I'm sure.

LEONARDO. I don't know.

MOTHER-IN-LAW. I understand his mother wasn't very pleased with
the idea.

LEONARDO. Maybe she's right. She's a slippery little thing.

WIFE. How can you be so nasty about such a good girl?

MOTHER-IN-LAW. (*Viciously.*) He's talking from experience. He
knows her well. She was *his* girl for three years. Didn't you
know that?

LEONARDO. But I finished with her. (*To his* WIFE.) Please, please, no tears! Stop your whining! (*Pulls her hands from her eyes.*) Come on, let's go and see the child.

(*They go out, arms round each other. A girl enters, full of enthusiasm.*)

MOTHER-IN-LAW. What are you so excited about?

GIRL. The groom came to the store and bought the best of everything there was.

MOTHER-IN-LAW. Did he come on his own?

GIRL. No, his mother was with him. A tall, serious lady. (*Imitates her.*) A proud and stylish lady.

MOTHER-IN-LAW. They have money.

GIRL. They bought the patterned stockings. You know the ones! The stockings we all dream of having. See! There's a swallow here [*points to the ankle*], a blue boat here [*her calf*], and here [*her thigh*] a rose. Beautiful! Perfect! A dream!

MOTHER-IN-LAW. Girl!

GIRL. A full, beautiful rose, with all the seeds and the firm stalk. And all, all in silk!

MOTHER-IN-LAW. The binding together of two good fortunes.

(*Enter* LEONARDO *and his* WIFE.)

GIRL. O let me tell you what they're buying at the shop!

LEONARDO. (*Loudly.*) Who gives a damn what they're buying?

WIFE. Let her talk.

MOTHER-IN-LAW. No need to be so nasty, Leonardo.

GIRL. (*Crying.*) I must go.

MOTHER-IN-LAW. Why do you always have to hurt people?

LEONARDO. Shut up!

MOTHER-IN-LAW. All right, then.

WIFE. (*To* LEONARDO.) What's wrong with you? Why are you so quick to anger? There's a storm in your mind. Tell me, tell me, what is it? I want to know. What's making you like this?

LEONARDO. Shut up. Stop it. Stop clawing at my mind.

WIFE. I won't stop. I want to know. I have a right to know. Look at me and Tell me. Now.

LEONARDO. (*Rising.*) Leave me alone.

WIFE. Where are you going, boy?

LEONARDO. Will you stop?

MOTHER-IN-LAW. (*To her daughter.*) Say no more. (LEONARDO *goes out.*) The child. The child.

(*She goes, comes back with child.* WIFE *stands absolutely still.*)

MOTHER-IN-LAW. The stallion's hooves are covered in blood
The stallion's mane is stiff as ice
And a broken silver knife
Hides behind the stallion's eyes.

They galloped down to the riverside
Galloped down where the water flowed
And though the water galloped fast
It couldn't touch his galloping blood.

WIFE. (*Dream-like.*) Sleep, carnation, you have no past,
The restless stallion drinks at last.

MOTHER-IN-LAW. Sleep, my rose, let troubles go.
The stallion's tears begin to flow.

WIFE. Sweet and peaceful be your sleep.

MOTHER-IN-LAW. The stallion, once, by the water's edge,
Would not drink deep.

WIFE. (*Firmly.*) Do not come in, stay away from here,
Gallop to the mountain now
And play your part,
Morning rears like a stallion above my head
And pain is a knife of ice
Stabbing my heart.

MOTHER-IN-LAW. (*Crying.*) Now my child is fast asleep.

WIFE. (*Crying.*) Sweet and peaceful, long and deep.

MOTHER-IN-LAW. Child, may the heavens bless your sleep,
The stallion still will not drink deep.

WIFE. (*Crying.*) Peace to your sleep, my perfect rose.
Who can say what the stallion knows?
Behind his eyes is a silver knife.
The stallion's tears begin to flow.
The river laughs at the stallion's eyes,
His cries are all I hear, his cries,
His never-ending cries...

[CURTAIN]

SCENE THREE

Interior of the cave where the BRIDE *lives. A cross of large rose-coloured flowers at the back. A caveroom. The round doors have lace curtains with rose-coloured tassels. Walls are whitish, with round fans, blue jars and little mirrors.*

SERVANT. (*Very friendly and full of humble hypocrisy.*) Come in, come in please.

(*Enter* BRIDEGROOM, *in black corduroy with a great golden chain, and the* MOTHER, *dressed in black satin, with a lace mantilla.*)

SERVANT. Please sit down. You won't have long to wait. They'll be here shortly.

(SERVANT *goes out.* MOTHER *and* BRIDEGROOM *sit stiffly.*)

MOTHER. We must get back home in time. This place is lost. How far away these people live.

BRIDEGROOM. This is good land.

MOTHER. Yes, but lost, isolated, alone like a man that never marries. It took us four hours to get here and not a house or a tree to be seen.

BRIDEGROOM. This is good land, but dry, dry.

MOTHER. Your father would have covered this place with the best of trees.

BRIDEGROOM. Without water?

MOTHER. He'd have searched until he found water. He hunted water with hunger and thirst in his heart. He planted ten cherry trees in the three years he was married to me. (*Remembering.*) He planted three walnut trees near the mill. He nourished a whole vineyard and a plant named Jupiter with blood-red flowers. But Jupiter dried up.

BRIDEGROOM. She must be getting ready, dressing herself.

(*Enter* FATHER *of the bride. He's old, white-haired. His head is bowed. They shake hands in silence.*)

FATHER. Were ye long on the road?

MOTHER. Four hours. (*They sit down.*)

FATHER. Ye must have taken the longest way possible.

MOTHER. I'm too old for that rough road by the river. That's a killing road.

BRIDEGROOM. That road makes her sick and giddy.

(*Pause.*)

FATHER. Good hemp harvest.

BRIDEGROOM. True.

FATHER. You have to fight with the land here. And the fight is never done. I had to attack this land, hurt it, punish it, make it lick its wounds until it co-operated. I had to punish it until it learned how to give.

MOTHER. Well, now it knows how to give. But I won't ask you for anything.

FATHER. You've come out of the fight better than me. You have rich vineyards. Each young vine is worth a silver coin. But I'm sorry that our lads are not...together, bound firmly together. I like binding things together. They're stronger that way, better for everyone concerned. I would give anything to bring your vineyards here and plant them there on the hillside. That would be perfect, the perfect joy of bringing together things that should be together.

BRIDEGROOM. And if they were together there wouldn't be so much work.

MOTHER. When I'm dead you can sell your land and buy land next to this hillside.

FATHER. No, never sell, never sell. Buy always, buy everything, buy until it seems there is no more left to buy. If I had sons, I'd have bought all the land I could. All this hill, right up to the source of the stream.

This is not good land, but willing hands can turn bad and indifferent to good and great. And since no people pass this way, the fruit is never stolen. You can sleep easy in your bed at night. Where there's no man there's no crime. (*Pause.*)

MOTHER. You know why I'm here.

FATHER. I do.

MOTHER. Well?

FATHER. I'm happy about it. They have talked it over.

MOTHER. My son's well off and he has a sensible head on his shoulders. He keeps an eye on things. He knows what's going on.

FATHER. I can say the same for my daughter.

MOTHER. He's good-looking, a fine strong body. He has never known a woman. His name is more spotless than a fresh sheet spread out in the sun.

FATHER. She's a good girl. She makes the best bread I've ever eaten. She knows how to keep her tongue quiet. She's soft and gentle and she'll work from dawn to dark with willing heart and hands. She embroiders well, and her strong teeth can cut a piece of string in two.

MOTHER. God bless her house.

FATHER. God bless her house.

(*Enter* SERVANT, *two trays, one with goblets, one with sweets.*)

MOTHER. (*To son.*) When do you want the wedding?

BRIDEGROOM. On Thursday.

FATHER. That's her twenty-second birthday.

MOTHER. Twenty-two years of age. If my eldest son had lived – twenty-two. He'd be alive now if men had not invented knives. A warm, living, working, laughing man – only for knives.

FATHER. Try to put it out of your mind.

MOTHER. Never. Always a hand on your breast.

FATHER. Thursday then. All right?

BRIDEGROOM. All right.

FATHER. You and I and the young couple will go to the church in a carriage. It's a long way from here. The guests will go in the carts and on horseback.

MOTHER. That's settled.

(*Enter* SERVANT.)

FATHER. Tell her it's time to come in.
(*To* MOTHER.) My heart will be happy if you like her.

(BRIDE *comes in. Modest; head bowed.*)

MOTHER. How do you feel? Happy?

BRIDE. Happy.

FATHER. No need to be so solemn. After all, she'll be your mother soon.

BRIDE. Happy. I said I'm happy. I meant it.

MOTHER. Of course you meant it. (*Takes her by the chin.*)
Come, look at me. Let me look at you.

FATHER. She's the living image of my wife.

MOTHER. Such a beautiful expression. You know what marriage means, child?

BRIDE. I do.

MOTHER. A man, children, and a wall that's two feet thick.

BRIDEGROOM. What more should I desire?

MOTHER. That your children should lead full, abundant lives.
Nothing else...desire that your children live.

BRIDE. I know what to do, what to desire.

MOTHER. Here are some gifts.

BRIDE. Thank you.

FATHER. Shall we have something?

MOTHER. No, thank you. (*To the* BRIDEGROOM.) And you?

BRIDEGROOM. Yes. (*He takes a sweet. The* BRIDE *does too.*)

FATHER.. (*To the* BRIDEGROOM.) Some wine?

MOTHER. No, he doesn't drink.

FATHER.. Good! (*They all stand.*)

BRIDEGROOM. I'll be here tomorrow.

BRIDE. When?

BRIDEGROOM. At five.

BRIDE. I'll see you then.

BRIDEGROOM. Whenever I leave you my heart is empty and a lump fills my throat.

BRIDE. When we're married you'll be all right.

BRIDEGROOM. Yes, yes, that's what I keep saying to myself.

MOTHER. Time to go, then. The sun waits for nobody. Is everything clear and agreed?

FATHER. Yes, everything is clear and agreed.

MOTHER. (*To the* SERVANT.) Goodbye, woman.

SERVANT. God's blessing on you both.

(*The* MOTHER *kisses the* BRIDE; *they begin to go quietly.*)

MOTHER. (*At the door.*) Goodbye. God bless you, daughter.

(*The* BRIDE *gestures goodbye.*)

FATHER. I'll take you to the road. (*They leave.*)

SERVANT. The presents! I'm bursting to see the presents!

BRIDE. (*Roughly.*) Don't touch them.

SERVANT. Let me see them!

BRIDE. No, I don't want to.

SERVANT. Let me see the stockings. I've heard they're really lovely. Let me see the stockings.

BRIDE. Didn't you hear me! I said no! I meant no!

SERVANT. What's wrong with you? Don't you want to see them? Don't you want to...It seems you don't even want to get married!

BRIDE. (*Bites her hand in anger.*) Oh!

SERVANT. Child! What's wrong? Are you bitter about giving up the life you have now? Don't be bitter. Come on, let's see the presents. (*She grabs the box.*)

BRIDE. (*Grips her wrists.*) Let go, blast you, let go.

SERVANT. Let me see them.

BRIDE. Let go, or I'll break your hand.

SERVANT. You're strong, stronger than a man.

BRIDE. I wish I was a man. (*Passionately.*) I wish I was a man. I can do a man's work, can't I? Why can't I be a man?

SERVANT. Why do you talk like that?

BRIDE. Shut up, you fool. Talk of something else.

(*The light fades. Long pause.*)

SERVANT. I heard a horse last night.

BRIDE. Did you? What time was it?

SERVANT. Three o'clock.

BRIDE. That horse must have strayed away from the herd in the darkness.

SERVANT. No, it didn't. This horse had a rider.

BRIDE. A rider? How can you tell?

SERVANT. I saw him. I saw him standing by your window. He frightened me.

BRIDE. Probably the man I'm going to marry. He sometimes comes to see me at that hour.

SERVANT. No, not him.

BRIDE. You saw the man?

SERVANT. Yes.

BRIDE. Who was it?

SERVANT. Leonardo.

BRIDE. (*Aggressively.*) You're lying! Why should Leonardo come here?

SERVANT. It *was* Leonardo. I *saw* Leonardo.

BRIDE. Shut up! Hold your damned tongue!

(*The sound of a horse comes clearly.*)

SERVANT. (*At the window.*) Come here! Come here! Look! Look! Is that the man?

BRIDE. Yes. Yes. That's him. That's the man.

[CURTAIN]

ACT TWO

SCENE ONE

Entry to BRIDE'S *house. Door at back. Night. Enter* BRIDE *in white ruffled petticoats, all laces, sleeveless white bodice.* SERVANT *similarly dressed.*

SERVANT. Your hair – let me finish combing it out here.

BRIDE. It's too hot in there.

SERVANT. In this place even the dawn is sticky with sweat.

(BRIDE *sits, looks in a hand mirror.* SERVANT *combs her hair.*)

BRIDE. In the place where my mother came from there were handsome, tall trees. And the land was rich.

SERVANT. She had a happy heart, bursting with joy.

BRIDE. But this place wasted her away to nothing.

SERVANT. That was her fate.

BRIDE. Our fate too – to waste away here. The very walls fling that terrible heat at us. Oh! You're hurting me!

SERVANT. I only want to bring out the best in your hair. I want it to fall like a graceful wave over your forehead.
(BRIDE *looks in mirror.*) You're beautiful, so beautiful. (*She kisses her hair.*)

BRIDE. (*Seriously.*) Just keep on combing.

SERVANT. You're a lucky woman, your life is blessed, you'll be able to kiss a man, hug him, caress him, feel the weight of his body on yours.

BRIDE. Shut up.

SERVANT. But the happiest moment of all will be whenever you wake up and feel him there beside you and his breath sweetly caresses your shoulders, soft as a nightingale's feather.

BRIDE. O be quiet!

SERVANT. But child, *what* does it *mean* to get married! Just that – nothing more! Is it the food, the drink, the day full of flowers? No, none of these. Marriage is a happy bed and a man and a woman, two becoming one. Imagine that! Two becoming one!

BRIDE. You shouldn't be talking like that.

SERVANT. Talking is a different matter; but it has its own magic. If we didn't talk, our dreams would drive us mad. Talk has its own happiness.

BRIDE. And its own misery.

SERVANT. I'm going to shift the orange blossoms from here to there so that the wreath will be a shining beauty on your hair. (*She tries on the orange blossoms.*)

BRIDE. (*Looks in mirror.*) Give me that. (*She takes the orange blossoms, looks, is utterly dejected, head falling.*)

SERVANT. What's wrong?

BRIDE. Let me be.

SERVANT. Don't be sad; this is no time to be sad. (*Brightly.*) Here, let me take it. (*The* BRIDE *flings the wreath away.*) Child, you are calling down God's wrath on you by flinging these orange-blossoms on the floor! Lift your head. You're getting married – remember! Do you want to get married? If you don't, say so. You can still pull out of it, even now. (BRIDE *gets up.*)

BRIDE. Black stormclouds. The icy knife of the wind cutting into my heart. Who hasn't felt it?

SERVANT. Do you love him?

BRIDE. I love him.

SERVANT. You love him, of course you love him.

BRIDE. But this is a huge step to take.

SERVANT. But it's a step you *must* take.

BRIDE. I've made my promise, given my word.

SERVANT. Let me put on the wreath.

BRIDE. Quick, then! They'll be here any minute.

SERVANT. They're on the road two hours already.

BRIDE. Is it far to the church from here?

SERVANT. Twenty miles by the river; twice as far by the road.

(BRIDE *gets up.* SERVANT *looks at her, excited, embraces her.*)

Open, open, shining Bride,
Open on your wedding day
The rivers of the world will bear
Your crown along the way.

BRIDE. (*Smiles.*) You!

SERVANT. (*Passionately kisses her.*)
Open
As the laurel-flower
Opens to the sun.
    Open
Near the young, strong laurel
Where love is won.
Be the flower opening, opening
Again, again.

(*Loud knocking.*)

BRIDE. Open! It must be the first guests.

SERVANT. (*Opens door, surprised.*) You!

LEONARDO. Me! Good morning.

SERVANT. The first one!

LEONARDO. Wasn't I invited?

SERVANT. Yes.

LEONARDO. Well then, here I am.

SERVANT. And your wife?

LEONARDO. She's coming in the mule-cart by the road. I came on horseback by the river.

SERVANT. Did you meet anyone?

LEONARDO. I passed several people.

SERVANT. You'll kill your horse if you ride him like that.

LEONARDO. If I ride him to death, well then he's dead.

(*Pause.*)

SERVANT. Sit down. There's nobody about.

LEONARDO. Where's the Bride?

SERVANT. I'm on my way to dress her.

LEONARDO. The Bride! This is her happy day!

SERVANT. (*Changes subject.*) The baby – how's the baby?

LEONARDO. What baby?

SERVANT. Your son.

LEONARDO. (*As if remembering a dream.*) Ah!

SERVANT. Will your son be here?

LEONARDO. No.

(*Pause. Then* VOICES *begin to sing far off.*)

VOICES. Awake, O bride, to you we sing
On this, your wedding morning.

LEONARDO. Awake, O bride, to you I sing
On this, your wedding morning.

SERVANT. The guests! The guests! But they're still quite a distance away.

LEONARDO. The bride will be wearing a big wreath of flowers, won't she? But it shouldn't be so big. A smaller one would suit her much better. Did the bridegroom bring the orange-blossom that she will wear on her breast?

BRIDE. (*Appears, petticoated, wearing wreath.*) Yes, he brought the blossoms.

SERVANT. What do you mean – coming out here like that?

BRIDE. O who cares? Why do you want to know about the orange blossom? Have you something else in mind?

LEONARDO. No, nothing else. What else could I possibly have in mind? (*Comes nearer.*) What else, I ask you, what else? You know me. Tell me this. What did I ever mean to you? Open up the locked box of your memory. Look into it. What did I mean to you? But what use were my two oxen and my shambles of a hut? That's the thorn in your side. What woman wants a poor man's passion?

BRIDE. Why did you come?

LEONARDO. To see your wedding.

BRIDE. Like I saw yours.

36

LEONARDO. You made it, fixed it with your own two hands. O they can kill me all right, but they can't spit on me. But gold and silver, silver and gold, though bright and shining, can sometimes spit with pure ferocity.

BRIDE. Liar!

LEONARDO. I'm not going to talk. I don't want to shout the truth aloud so that the very hills will blush to hear it.

BRIDE. I can shout louder than you.

SERVANT. Stop, stop talking like this. (*To the* BRIDE.) There's no need to talk about the past. (*The* SERVANT *looks uneasily about her.*)

BRIDE. She's right. Why am I talking to you, now, even now? But it galls me that you should ride out here to spy on me and on my wedding, and talk about the orange blossom with God-knows-what on your mind. Go outside the door; wait there for your wife.

LEONARDO. Talk to me. Talk to me.

SERVANT. (*In fury.*) No talk, no talk.

LEONARDO. From the first moment of my marriage I've spent nights and days thinking about whose fault it was. Every thought leads to a different thought, and every old fault gives birth to a new one. And when I think I've seen them all, yet another fault springs up like a crisp black flower of evil to astonish and disturb my mind. I live under a cloud of madness – sleeping, waking, walking or on horseback.

BRIDE. A man like you who's not afraid to ride a horse to death needn't give a second thought to riding roughshod over a girl stuck somewhere out in the wilds of the desert. But if you have your horse I have my pride. And that's why I'm getting married today. I'll lock myself away with my husband and love him, nobody but him.

LEONARDO. Pride is pointless, useless. (*Comes nearer.*)

BRIDE. Don't come near me!

LEONARDO. To burn with passionate desire, and not to speak of it, is the most atrocious punishment we can inflict on ourselves. Pride! What did pride ever do for me – alone in my heart – not seeing you – knowing you were lying awake night after night after night? Pride is worse than useless – it only brought the red-hot coals of despair raining and flaming down on my head. You think that time can heal love's wounds and that walls will hide love's cries; it isn't true, it isn't true! When wounds and cries are buried so deeply in the darkness of my heart, nothing on God's earth can change them, or pull them back into the light where wounds may be cured and cries heard.

BRIDE. (*Trembling.*) Your voice! I mustn't listen to your voice! I feel as if I were drunk and had fallen asleep all wrapped in a silken quilt of roses. I'm being dragged down, I'm drowning, I know I'm drowning, but I'm lost and trembling and I plunge on down and down...

SERVANT. (*Seizing* LEONARDO *by lapels.*) Get out! Go away! You *must* go away!

LEONARDO. This is the last time I'll ever speak to her. There's nothing to be afraid of.

BRIDE. I know I'm out of my mind and I know my breasts rot with longing for him – but look at me, here I am, my heart at peace because I hear him, because my eyes follow the lovely movements of his arms and hands.

LEONARDO. My heart can never know peace until I tell you what's in it. I got married. Now you're getting married.

SERVANT. Yes, yes, she *is* getting married. *Married*, you understand?

(VOICES *sing, nearer now.*)

VOICES. Awake, O bride, to you we sing
On this your wedding morning.

BRIDE. Awake, O bride, awake.
(*She runs towards her room.*)

SERVANT. The guests are here now.
(*To* LEONARDO.) Stay away from her!

LEONARDO. Don't worry. (*Goes out. Day begins to break.*)

FIRST GIRL. (*Entering.*)
Awake, O Bride, awake now
Your wedding is at hand,

Sing and dance and may your wreath
Of orange blossom bless the land.

VOICES. Awake, dear Bride, lift up your head.
Tonight you grace the marriage-bed.

SERVANT. (*Getting herself going.*)
Open
As the laurel-flower
Opens to the sun.
Open
Near the young, strong laurel
Where love is won.
Be the flower opening, opening
Again, again.

SECOND GIRL. (*Entering.*)
Now is the moment to awaken.
See her long hair
Beautifully falling down.
Snowy petticoat, silver, leather boots,
And on her head a jasmine crown.

SERVANT. Shepherdess so calm and caring
The shy moon grows daring, daring.

FIRST GIRL. If any man would dare be mine,
Leave your hat under the vine.

FIRST YOUTH. (*Enters, holding high his hat.*)
Bride, awaken,
Welcome the wedding-guests,
Shower welcome-words on every head.
They come laughing, generous
With dahlias piled high on trays
And wholesome loaves of bread.

VOICES. Let the bride awaken now.
Love smiles and ripens on the bough.

SECOND GIRL. The crown of flowers
Is proud on the bride's head.
Golden lace has its own power.
The bridegroom moves. The crown is tied.

SERVANT. The sleepless bride will be
Restless under the orange tree.

THIRD GIRL. (*Entering*.)
The bridegroom's flawless gifts of love
Add splendour to the orange-grove.

(*Three* GUESTS *come in.*)

FIRST YOUTH. Awaken, gentle dove.
Harsh bells of night
Are gentle in the morning light.

GUEST. Bride, crown of flowers on her head:
Virgin of morning,
Tonight, a wife in bed.

FIRST GIRL. Dark girl, flowery crown,
No one escapes the spell
Rustling in your silken gown.

GUEST. Dark girl, facing oath and vow,
Even the cold dewy morning
Pays homage to you now.

FIRST YOUTH. Dark girl, virgin, come awake.
Hearts like orange blossoms shake.

SERVANT. I would write upon the wind
I would write on every tree
The words 'God grant you happy children
And may your life all blessed be.'

VOICES. Let the bride awaken now.
Love smiles and ripens on the bough.

FIRST YOUTH. This morning – she marries!

GUEST. This morning – she marries!
Never, never before
Did such a dream of a girl
Leave her father's door.
Here is the morning's smiling bride,
Her happy captain by her side.

FATHER. (*Entering*.) Yes, she is a captain's wife.
Now let the captain come
And bear away his treasure
On the strong backs of his oxen.

THIRD GIRL. A golden flower –
That's what I call the bridegroom.
And where he walks the land becomes
A flowery kingdom.

SERVANT. O my lucky girl.

SECOND YOUTH. Awaken, bride.

SERVANT. O my shapely girl.

FIRST GIRL. Every window gives a shout of joy
For the wedding, for the wedding.

SECOND GIRL. Let the bride step out.

FIRST GIRL. Come out, come out.

SERVANT. Let the bells ring, let the bells
Sing and shout
And fling their voices all about.

FIRST YOUTH. Here she comes! Here she comes!
The bride is coming here at last!

SERVANT. Like a huge bull, the wedding
Stirs and rises
In the fields of morning.

(*The* BRIDE *appears, dressed in a black dress of 1900 style with a bustle and long train of pleated gauze and heavy lace. An orange-blossom wreath crowns her hair. Sound of guitars. The* GIRLS *kiss the* BRIDE.)

THIRD GIRL. What perfume have you got in your hair?

BRIDE. (*Laughs.*) None.

SECOND GIRL. The cloth – it's out of this world.

FIRST YOUTH. Here's the groom.

BRIDEGROOM. Welcome.

FIRST GIRL. (*Putting a flower behind his ear.*)
A flower of gold –
That's what I call the bridegroom.

SECOND GIRL. Flower of gold –
His eyes tell stories of pure joy
No man has ever told.

(*The* GROOM *goes to the* BRIDE.)

BRIDE. Why are you wearing these shoes?

BRIDEGROOM. I prefer them to the black ones – they're bright and cheerful.

LEONARDO'S WIFE. (*Enters, kisses the* BRIDE.) Good luck, God's blessing. Good health.

(*Excited talk all round.*)

LEONARDO. (*Like a man doing his duty.*)
This morning you will marry
and this flowery crown you'll wear.

WIFE. And all the fields are happy
When the dew falls from your hair.

MOTHER. (*To the father.*) Are these people here as well?

FATHER. Yes, they're part of the family. Today is a day for forgiveness.

MOTHER. I'll tolerate this, but I won't forgive.

BRIDEGROOM. Your wreath is beautiful. The sight of you fills me with joy.

BRIDE. It's time to go to the church. Quick.

BRIDEGROOM. You seem to be in a hurry.

BRIDE. Yes, I want to be your wife now, straightaway, without delay, so that I can be with you alone, and hear no other voice but yours.

BRIDEGROOM. That's what I want too!

BRIDE. And I want to see only your eyes, yours alone. And I want you to hold me so firmly in your arms that if my dead mother called me, I couldn't pull myself away from you.

BRIDEGROOM. I have strong arms. I'll hold you for fifty years and never let you go!

BRIDE. (*Taking his arm, dramatically.*) Hold me forever!

FATHER. Quickly! Quickly! Make ready the mules and the carts! Let's go! The sun is up!

MOTHER. Drive carefully. And pray that nothing goes wrong.

(*In the background the great door opens.*)

42

SERVANT. (*Crying.*) Bride, as you leave this house
Remember that you are
More shining and alive
Than any heavenly star.

FIRST GIRL. Your body is clean,
Clean is your dress.
God is pleased to see you
And gives you His blessing.

(*They start to leave.*)

SECOND GIRL. Now you leave your house for good
And you seek the house of God.

SERVANT. The wind is excited and
Scatters flowers in the sand.

THIRD GIRL. Young girl, young girl,
White as sunlight.

SERVANT. The lace of her mantilla –
Cold dark winds that make me shiver.

(*They leave. Sounds of guitars, castanets, tambourines.* LEONARDO *and
his* WIFE *are left alone.*)

WIFE. Let's go.

LEONARDO. Where?

WIFE. The church. But you're not going on horseback. You're
coming with me.

LEONARDO. In the mule-cart?

WIFE. Of course.

LEONARDO. I'm not a man to travel by mule-cart.

WIFE. I'm not a woman to go to a wedding without her husband.
I'm not going to put up with this any longer!

LEONARDO. Neither will I!

WIFE. Why are you looking at me like that? Your eyes are wicked
thorns.

LEONARDO. Let's go.

WIFE. What's happening? I don't know. I'm trying to think, and I can't think. But there's one thing I do know. You have ditched me, cast me aside. But I am the mother of your son. And there's another on the way. And that's exactly how things stand. My mother found herself in the same awful situation. Well, I'm not stirring from here.

(VOICES *outside*.)

(VOICES). As you set out from home
To reach the church that seems so far
Remember you are brighter
Than the light of any star.

WIFE. (*Crying*.) Remember you are brighter than
The light of any star.

I remember I left my home too – just like her. They could have packed the whole damned countryside into my mouth, I was so gaping with trust.

LEONARDO. Let's go.

WIFE. With me?

LEONARDO. Yes. (*Pause*.) Well, let's go. (*They leave*.)

VOICES. As you set out from home
To reach the church that seems so far
Remember you are brighter
Thank the light of any star.

[SLOW CURTAIN]

SCENE TWO

Outside the cave-house of the BRIDE. *White, grey, blue tones. Plains in background, dark. Everything hard as if in ceramics.*

SERVANT. (*Arranging glasses and trays on table.*)
Turning,
The wheel was turning,
The water was flowing
And here is the wedding night.
May the branches part
And the moon shine with pride
On her white balcony
All through the throbbing night.

(*Loudly.*) Put on the tablecloths.

(*Lyrically.*) Singing,
Bride and groom were singing
And the water was flowing
And here is the wedding night.
Rime-frost, flash and vanish,
Bitter almonds, fill with honey
Till your flesh is sweet.

(*Loudly.*) Prepare the wine.

(*Lyrically.*) O beautiful girl
Most beautiful of all
The water is flowing,
Your wedding-night's coming.
Hold in your skirts
Stay in your house
Your man is a dove
With his heart on fire.
The fields are waiting
For the fresh blood spurting.
Turning,
The wheel was turning,
The water was flowing
And here is your wedding night.
O water, water,
Sparkle and shine
Like the world's first light.

MOTHER. (*Entering.*) At last.

FATHER. Are we the first?

SERVANT. No, Leonardo and his wife were the first. They drove like mad devils. The wife was stiff with terror. They came here as if they were on horseback.

FATHER. That fellow is just looking for trouble. There's bad blood in his veins.

MOTHER. What blood do you expect? He has the same bad blood everyone in his family has. That same blood was in his great-grandfather, a killer, and it has flowed through the veins of the different generations of men in that family – an evil breed, always with knives on their bodies and lying smiles on their faces, happy only when they're killing something, destroying what others sweat and labour to create. The devil's blood is in them.

FATHER. Enough said!

SERVANT. But how – how can enough be said?

MOTHER. I'm hurt in the marrow of my bones, in the depth of my veins. On the forehead of every man in that family I see only the hand that killed what belonged to me. Look at me! Do you think I'm mad? If I am, it's because I haven't screamed out all the rage that's in me. How can I ever scream that rage? In here, right here in my heart, there's a scream clamouring to be heard, and every moment of my life I have to beat down that scream, stifle it, imprison it under my shawl. But my dead have been taken from me and I have to hold my tongue. And then, of course, people are quick to judge and blame. (*She takes off her shawl.*)

FATHER. Today is not the day to be calling these things to mind.

MOTHER. When people start to talk of it, I have to say my say. And especially today. Because today is the day that I will be left alone in my own house. My last son is gone.

FATHER. But you can look forward to having others with you in the future.

MOTHER. That's what I'd love: grandchildren.

(*They sit down.*)

FATHER. I hope they have children in plenty. This land needs workers that don't have to be hired. This land need fighters – fighters against weeds, thistles, rocks that come from God alone knows where; and stones, endless, endless stones that would break your heart if you gave in to them. And these workers with the hearts of warriors must belong to the house, must be powerful and patient, must kill the weeds and grow the seeds. Sons! Only sons can work like that! God send them son after son after son.

MOTHER. And may they have daughters too! Men are like the wind. Wherever men go you'll find knives and guns. Girls don't wander the streets like that.

FATHER. I hope... (*Happily.*) I believe they'll have both. Sons and daughters. Daughters and sons.

MOTHER. My son will plant good seed in her. His father before him had the best of seed. He could have had many sons with me.

FATHER. Do you know what I'd like? I'd like if he could have three sons in one day! That'd be a great start!

MOTHER. It takes longer than that. It takes a long time, long years. That's why the blood of one's own son spilled on the ground is such a terrible sight. A fountain of blood gushed forth in a minute but it cost years of my life. When I reached my son he lay stretched out in the middle of the street. I covered my hands with his blood, I put my hands in my mouth, I licked his blood with my tongue because it was my blood, my own blood. You'll never know what that's like. And the earth that was soaked by his blood, I'd pack that earth in a chalice of glass and topaz.

FATHER. Hope now. Let your heart be hope. My daughter has wide hips and your son is strong.

MOTHER. That's why my heart is full of hope.

(*They rise.*)

FATHER. Are the trays of wheat ready?

SERVANT. Yes, they're ready.

WIFE. (*Entering.*) May good luck smile on everyone today – and tomorrow!

47

MOTHER. Thank you.

LEONARDO. Will there be a celebration?

FATHER. Yes, a small one. People can't stay for long.

SERVANT. Here they come!

(*Enter guests in happy groups.* BRIDE *and* GROOM *enter arm-in-arm.* LEONARDO *leaves.*)

BRIDEGROOM. What a wedding! So many people!

BRIDE. (*Sullen.*) Indeed.

FATHER. It was fabulous.

MOTHER. Entire branches of families came along.

BRIDEGROOM. People who never left their own houses before came to see us today, to wish us well.

MOTHER. Your father sowed good seed. For you, the harvest is rich.

BRIDEGROOM. There were cousins of mine there and I'd never met them before.

MOTHER. People came from the farms near the sea.

BRIDEGROOM. (*Happy.*) They were really frightened of the horses.

(*They talk.*)

MOTHER. (*To* BRIDE.) What's on your mind?

BRIDE. Nothing much.

MOTHER. Your life is blessed but your heart is heavy.

(*Sound of guitars.*)

BRIDE. Like lead.

MOTHER. Your blessings shouldn't weigh on you like that. You should be as happy as a dove.

BRIDE. Are you staying tonight?

MOTHER. No. There's no one at home.

BRIDE. You should stay.

FATHER. (*To the* MOTHER.) Look at the dancers. They're forming dances of the distant seashore.

(LEONARDO *enters and sits, his* WIFE *stands behind him, stiff.*)

MOTHER. Dancers, did you say? They're cousins of my husband. They're stiff as pokers when it comes to dancing.

FATHER. Ah, I like watching them! It's a joy, a welcome change in this house! (*He leaves.*)

BRIDEGROOM. (*To* BRIDE.) Did you like the orange blossoms?

BRIDE. (*Looks strangely at him.*) Yes.

BRIDEGROOM. Good. They're made of wax. They'll last forever. I'd love if you'd had them all over your dress.

BRIDE. There's no need for that.

(LEONARDO *goes off to the right.*)

FIRST GIRL. Come on, let's take your pins out.

BRIDE. (*To* GROOM.) I'll be right back.

WIFE. I hope you'll be happy with my cousin.

BRIDEGROOM. I will. Of course I will.

WIFE. Nobody here but the two of you. Staying here, never going out, making a home, rearing a family. I wish I too could live far away in a place like this!

BRIDEGROOM. You should buy land. Mountain land is cheap and it's easy to rear the children.

WIFE. We've no money. And the way things are going – !

BRIDEGROOM. Your husband is a great worker.

WIFE. Yes, but he's always on the go, flitting from one thing to another. He has no patience.

SERVANT. Aren't you tasting anything? I'm giving some wine-cakes to your mother. She adores them.

BRIDEGROOM. Get three dozen for her.

WIFE. No, no! Half-a-dozen is quite enough for her!

BRIDEGROOM. But today is special – it'll never happen again!

WIFE. (*To* SERVANT.) Where's Leonardo?

SERVANT. Probably with the guests.

WIFE. I'll go and see.

(*She leaves.*)

SERVANT. (*Looking off at dance.*) That dance is so beautiful! So beautiful!

BRIDEGROOM. Why aren't you dancing?

SERVANT. Nobody asked me.

(TWO GIRLS *cross at back. During this scene, there's a lot of such lively movement.*)

BRIDEGROOM. Young men are pig-ignorant. Old stagers like you are better dancers than the bright young things.

SERVANT. Well, fancy that! A compliment! From you! Why, you're talking like a man! And why not? What a family you belong to! Great men, great men! I was only a little girl when I saw your grandfather getting married. There was a man! What a fine figure of a man! It was as though a mountain was chasing a mate!

BRIDEGROOM. I'm not as tall as him.

SERVANT. But you have the same lively sparkle in your eye. Where's the girl?

BRIDEGROOM. Taking off her wreath.

SERVANT. Look! Since you'll not be sleeping by midnight, I got some delicious ham for you and a good supply of the best old wine. You'll find it in the cupboard, on the lower shelf. You may be needing it.

BRIDEGROOM. (*Smiling.*) I don't think so. I'll not be eating at midnight.

SERVANT. (*Slyly.*) Well if you don't need it, maybe your wife will. Making love can be tiring work!

(*She leaves.*)

FIRST YOUTH. (*Entering.*) Please come and have a drink with us. You *must* come and drink with us.

BRIDEGROOM. (*Entering.*) I'm looking for my wife.

SECOND YOUTH. O you'll have her near dawn!

FIRST YOUTH. That's the best time for it!

SECOND YOUTH. Just for a minute, one little minute!

BRIDEGROOM. All right, let's go.

(*They leave. Great excitement heard. Enter the* BRIDE. *The* TWO GIRLS *rush to meet her from the opposite side.*)

FIRST GIRL. Who did you give the first pin to: me or this one?

BRIDE. I don't know. I can't remember.

FIRST GIRL. You gave it to me, you gave it to me, right here.

SECOND GIRL. You gave it to me, standing in front of the altar.

BRIDE. (*Upset, uneasy.*) I can't say for sure. I don't remember.

FIRST GIRL. O I wish that you would –

BRIDE. (*Interrupts.*) Look, I don't care. I've a lot to think about besides a pin.

SECOND GIRL. I'm sorry. I'm sorry.

(LEONARDO *crosses at back.*)

BRIDE. (*Sees* LEONARDO.) This is a hard time for me!

FIRST GIRL. We wouldn't know anything about that.

BRIDE. You'll know plenty about it when your turn comes. This is a very hard thing to do.

FIRST GIRL. Are you hurt? Angry?

BRIDE. No. Forgive me.

SECOND GIRL. What for? But the two pins are good for getting married, aren't they?

BRIDE. Yes, yes, they both are.

FIRST GIRL. I wonder which of us will be married first?

BRIDE. Why are you so worked up about it?

SECOND GIRL. Well, we are.

BRIDE. Why?

FIRST GIRL. Well...

(*She kisses the* SECOND GIRL. *They run off. Enter* BRIDEGROOM *slowly, kisses bride from behind.*)

BRIDE. (*In fright.*) Stop! Stop! Don't touch me!

BRIDEGROOM. Are you afraid of me?

BRIDE. O it's you!

BRIDEGROOM. Who else?
  (*Pause.*)
  Me. Or your father. Who else?

BRIDE. That's right.

BRIDEGROOM. Your father would have been more gentle.

BRIDE. (*Darkly.*) Of course. Naturally.

BRIDEGROOM. (*Embracing her rather roughly.*) Your father is an old man. Old.

BRIDE. Let me go! Stop it!

BRIDEGROOM. Why?
  (*Lets her go.*)

BRIDE. People...the people can see us.

(*The* SERVANT *crosses at back without looking at* BRIDE *and* GROOM.)

BRIDEGROOM. So what? We're married now, aren't we?

BRIDE. Yes, but we'll be...just wait...later!

BRIDEGROOM. What's wrong? You look frightened.

BRIDE. O I'm all right. Don't leave, don't go.

(*Enter Leonardo's* WIFE.)

WIFE. I didn't mean to intrude...

BRIDEGROOM. What do you want?

WIFE. Did my husband come this way?

BRIDEGROOM. No.

WIFE. I can't find him anywhere, and his horse is gone from the stable.

BRIDEGROOM. (*Happily.*) He's gone.

(*The* WIFE *leaves, upset. Enter* SERVANT.)

SERVANT. You two must be very happy with all the blessings and good wishes pouring on you from all sides.

BRIDEGROOM. I wish it were all over now. My wife is getting tired.

SERVANT. What's wrong, child?

BRIDE. I feel as if I'd been hit on the head!

SERVANT. A wife out of our mountains has to stay strong! (*To the* GROOM.) She's yours now. Cure her.

(*She leaves, running away.*)

BRIDEGROOM. (*Embracing, kissing her.*) Come on, let's dance.

BRIDE. No, I'd rather stretch out in bed for a while.

BRIDEGROOM. I'll go with you.

BRIDE. No, never! With all these people still here? What would they think? These people – so many people. I'd love to be alone for a while. Please leave me alone.

BRIDEGROOM. All right. I'll leave you alone now. But not tonight.

BRIDE. Tonight will be different. (BRIDE *leaves.*)

BRIDEGROOM. That's what I like to hear.

(*The* MOTHER *comes in.*)

MOTHER. Son.

BRIDEGROOM. And where have you been?

MOTHER. Out there, with the people, in the middle of all the noise. Are you all right?

BRIDEGROOM. Yes.

MOTHER. Your wife – where is she?

BRIDEGROOM. Taking a rest. It's a bad day for brides.

MOTHER. Bad day? It's good. The best. On that day I became myself. I was rich. I grew to know myself.

(*Enter the* SERVANT. *Goes towards* BRIDE'S *room.*)

MOTHER. It was like opening up new ground or planting young trees in the earth.

BRIDEGROOM. Are you leaving?

MOTHER. Yes, I should be at home.

BRIDEGROOM. Alone.

MOTHER. No, not alone. My head is clamouring with thoughts and memories. Men. Fights. Knives, big and small.

BRIDEGROOM. Fights that aren't fights any more.

(*Enter* SERVANT *quickly. She disappears at back, running.*)

MOTHER. As long as you live, you have to fight.

BRIDEGROOM. As long as I live, I'll do what you say.

MOTHER. Love her. Always try to love your wife and if she's acting bitchy or foolish or mean, give her the kind of love that hurts a bit: a rough hug, a bite, and then follow that with a gentle kiss. When you do this, do it in a way that doesn't make her angry but in such a way that she'll know for sure that you're the man, the ruler, the boss, the one who gives the orders and expects to be obeyed without question. I learned all this from your father. But he's dead and gone from you, and I must be his voice, and I must tell you what to do so that you'll be the master of your house and the king of your land.

BRIDEGROOM. As long as I live, I'll do what you say.

FATHER. (*Enters.*) Where's my daughter?

BRIDEGROOM. She's lying down.

(*The* FATHER *goes to look for her.*)

FIRST GIRL. Where's the bride and groom? We want to dance with them!

FIRST YOUTH. (*To the* GROOM.) You must lead the dance!

FATHER. (*Enters.*) She's not there.

BRIDEGROOM. No?

FATHER. She's probably gone out on the balcony.

BRIDEGROOM. I'll see. (*Goes out. Excitement; guitars.*)

FIRST GIRL. They've started the dance already. (*Leaves.*)

BRIDEGROOM. (*Enters.*) She's not there.

MOTHER. (*Uneasily.*) She's not?

FATHER. Where is she? Where's she gone?

SERVANT. Where is she? Where is she?

MOTHER. We don't know.

(GROOM *leaves. Enter three guests.*)

FATHER. (*Worried.*) The dance – is she at the dance?

SERVANT. No, she's not at the dance.

FATHER. (*More worried.*) There's an awful lot of people out there. Look for her!

SERVANT. I've looked already. She's not there!

FATHER. (*Alarmed.*) Where is she? Where is she?

BRIDEGROOM. (*Enters.*) I can't find her anywhere. I've looked and looked but she's nowhere to be found.

MOTHER. (*To the* FATHER.) Where is your daughter?

(*Leonardo's* WIFE *enters.*)

WIFE. They've gone! Gone! They've run away together! Run away! On horseback! Their arms around each other – herself and Leonardo – galloping away like lightning, lightning.

FATHER. No, it can't be true! Not my daughter!

MOTHER. Yes, yes, your daughter! The treacherous chit of a wicked mother, herself the devil's bitch. But your daughter is my son's wife!

BRIDEGROOM. Let's go after them! A horse, give me a horse!

MOTHER. Who has a horse? Now! Who has a horse? Whoever has a horse will get everything I have – my eyes, my hands, my tongue –

VOICE. I have a horse.

MOTHER. (*To the* BRIDEGROOM.) Go after them! Get them!

(*He leaves with two young men.*)

No, stay! Don't go! His breed – they're all killers – they kill sharp and clean and quick – but yes, go, go, go, and I'll follow you!

FATHER. Not my daughter! Not my daughter! Maybe she's thrown herself down the well.

MOTHER. Only decent women throw themselves down wells! Not that thing! But she's my son's wife now! (*Looks around.*) Two crowds! There are two crowds here!

(*They all enter.*)

Two crowds! My family and your family! Together now! Set out from here! Find them! Shake this wedding from your bones, shake all this food and music from your bones, and find them! Together now! Help my son!

(*The people separate into two sections.*)

He has the backing of his whole family. He has his cousins from the seashore, and he has his gang of inland people too. Out! Out of here! Take every road! The wedding's over! It's the time for blood again! Two crowds of us, two bonded families. You lead yours. I lead mine. Go! After them! Follow them! To the killing end of the earth, if you must!

[CURTAIN]

ACT THREE

SCENE ONE

Forest at night. Huge, humid trunks of trees. Dark atmosphere. Two violins are heard.

(*Enter* THREE WOODCUTTERS.)

FIRST WOODCUTTER. Did they find them?

SECOND WOODCUTTER. Not yet, but they're scouring every hole and corner for them.

THIRD WOODCUTTER. They'll find them in no time.

SECOND WOODCUTTER. Eh-h-h?

THIRD WOODCUTTER. Eh?

SECOND WOODCUTTER. They seem to be coming nearer to us on all the roads at the same time.

FIRST WOODCUTTER. The moon'll be up soon. That'll help them to find them.

SECOND WOODCUTTER. I think they should let them go free.

FIRST WOODCUTTER. It's a wide world. Plenty room in it for every-one.

THIRD WOODCUTTER. They'll kill them.

SECOND WOODCUTTER. A man must follow his heart's desire. They did the right thing to run away.

FIRST WOODCUTTER. Ah they were only deceiving each other, the pair o' fools! But the hot blood had its way in the heel o' the hunt.

THIRD WOODCUTTER. Blood! Hot blood!

FIRST WOODCUTTER. You have to follow the blood, the road pointed out by the blood.

SECOND WOODCUTTER. We work a thirsty earth. And this thirsty old earth drinks any blood that escapes. Any blood!

FIRST WOODCUTTER. So what? I'd rather be dead with the blood drained out of me than going around like an upright corpse with the blood rotting in my veins.

THIRD WOODCUTTER. Easy!

FIRST WOODCUTTER. Eh? Can you hear something?

THIRD WOODCUTTER. Crickets, frogs, the packed, mad assassins of the night. Darkness waiting in ambush, murder in its heart.

FIRST WOODCUTTER. But the horse – do you hear the horse?

THIRD WOODCUTTER. No.

FIRST WOODCUTTER. He must be making love to her now.

SECOND WOODCUTTER. Her body is his; his body is hers.

THIRD WOODCUTTER. They'll find them; they'll kill them.

FIRST WOODCUTTER. The blood of their love will have flowed into each other by then. They'll be drained, spent. Two empty cups. Two rivers run dry.

SECOND WOODCUTTER. Plenty cloud tonight. The moon might not break through. Nothing like clouds to make a prisoner of the moon.

THIRD WOODCUTTER. Moon or no moon, the bridegroom will find them out. I saw him leaving. He was like a star gone mad. His face was ashes. All the dead of his family were gathered in his eyes. Nothing like the dead to galvanise the living.

FIRST WOODCUTTER. The dead of his family were lying in their blood in the middle of the street.

SECOND WOODCUTTER. That's it!

THIRD WOODCUTTER. Blood-lovers! Do you think they'll be able to break through the circle?

SECOND WOODCUTTER. It'll go hard with them. They're surrounded by knives and guns, knives and guns everywhere for forty miles around. A forest of knives.

THIRD WOODCUTTER. He's riding a good horse.

SECOND WOODCUTTER. Carrying a woman, though.

FIRST WOODCUTTER. We're nearly there now.

SECOND WOODCUTTER. A big tree with forty strong branches. Ah but we'll soon knock it!

THIRD WOODCUTTER. The moon is starting to come out. We'd better hurry.

(*A brightness from left.*)

FIRST WOODCUTTER. Moon stealing out from the clouds!
Moonlight touching the great leaves.

SECOND WOODCUTTER. Let jasmine fill and thrill the blood!

FIRST WOODCUTTER. Moon, lonely moon,
Astray among the leaves.

SECOND WOODCUTTER. Silver light on the bride's face.

THIRD WOODCUTTER. Old moon, grinning in your tricky evil,
Steal a shadow from a branch
As a gift for their bloody love.

(*They leave. The* MOON *appears, shining brightly on left. The* MOON *is a pale young woodcutter. The stage takes on an intense blue radiance.*)

MOON. I shine with loneliness and I'm looking for love.
The world is a swan,
Shrewd swan in the river,
A cathedral's eye,
False light on the leaves,
There's no escape for love.
I am everything I see.
The eyes of love are mesmerised by me.
Who is hiding? Who is hiding?
And who is crying
In the grieving shadows of the valley?
The moon is a knife
Alone in the air,
A steely threat to love,
Cause of the blood's pain.
Let me in! Let me in!
Freezing I drift down
To your walls and windows.
Roofs, open! Breasts, open!
Let me in! Let me in!
Let me warm myself against your skin.
I am cold! I am cold!
My ashes of sleeping steel and iron
Yearn for the climax of the fire

On top of every mountain
In the twist of every street.
But the snow is a thief
And it steals me away
On the flawless broad of its back
And I fall, and I soak
Into water mercilessly cold.
Then I'm a corpse
On the icy broad of my back
But tonight there will be
Red blood in my cheeks,
Red blood for the reeds
That gather and whine at the feet of the wind.
Let there be neither
Shadow nor shelter,
No escape for love,
No escape for love.
Let me lie at a breast
Where my old heart is warm.
A heart! I'm a heart!
I'm blood, I'm a heart, and I'm living
And beating, repeating
Myself in love.
Warm! Let my heart
Break out through my chest,
My flesh rebel at itself,
My head whirl and spin,
Break out through my mountains,
Out through my cold.
Let me in! Let me in!

(*To the branches.*)

I will banish all shadows.
I will penetrate everywhere.
Even among the dark, forbidding trees
I will throw my shining knives of light
So that my choking ice will melt
And this night there will be
Blood
To electrify my flesh,
Blood
To thrill my cheek,

Blood
For the reeds that gather and whine
At the feet of the wind.
Who is hiding? Who is hiding?
Out, I say. Follow them, I say.
They will not get away.
They must not get away.
I will search every road
Until I find them.
I will plant in the horse's blood
A fever raging bright as diamonds.
I shine with loneliness and I'm looking for love.

(*He disappears among the tree trunks; the stage returns to the dark lighting. A* BEGGAR WOMAN *comes out, covered in dark green cloth, barefoot. We can barely see her face. This character does not appear in the cast.*)

BEGGAR WOMAN. The moon is going away
    Just when they're coming near.
    They'll not get out of here.
    The whispering river and the whispering trees
    Will conspire together to stifle
    The wounded flight of their screams.
    It will happen here
    And quickly.
    I'm worn out, fit to drop.
    The coffins are ready,
    The white sheets wait on the bedroom floor
    For heavy bodies with ripped throats.
    Let all the birds sleep,
    Let not even a single bird awaken,
    Let the breeze gather their death-cries
    In the folds of her skirt
    And fly with them
    Over the black tree-tops
    Or bury them
    In white mud.

    (*Impatiently.*) Oh that moon! That moon!

(*The moon appears. Intense light again.*)

MOON. They're coming. One crowd through the ravine and the other by the road near the river. I'm going to throw light on the rocks and stones. What do you need?

63

BEGGAR WOMAN. Nothing.

MOON. The wind is cutting now, like a two-bladed knife.

BEGGAR WOMAN. Throw your light on the waistcoat
    And open the buttons.
    The knives will find their own way after that.

MOON. Let death come slowly to them
    Like a shy friend.
    Let their blood slide
    Hissing and delicate
    Between my fingers.
    Open your eyes; see my ashen valleys
    Opening in longing
    For blood,
    For the hot uncontainable blood of love,
    Gushing from their trembling bodies.

BEGGAR WOMAN. We must try to stop them
    Getting past the stream.
    Be still!

MOON. There they are! (*Leaves. Stage is dark.*)

BEGGAR WOMAN. Light! Light! Lots of light!
    Can you hear me?
    They can't get away.

(*Enter* GROOM *and* FIRST YOUTH. *The* BEGGAR WOMAN *sits, covers herself with her cloak.*)

BRIDEGROOM. This way.

FIRST YOUTH. You'll not find them.

BRIDEGROOM. (*In anger.*) I will. I'll find them.

FIRST YOUTH. I think they've gone another way.

BRIDEGROOM. No, just a minute ago, my blood heard that galloping horse.

FIRST YOUTH. It could have been another horse.

BRIDEGROOM. (*Savagely.*) Listen, boy. There's only one horse in the whole world – his. Do you understand that? Now, if you're going to follow me, don't say another word.

FIRST YOUTH. I just want to –

BRIDEGROOM. Not a word out of you! I know I'll find them here. Do you see this hand? It's not my hand! It's my brother's hand, my father's hand, the hand of all the dead men in my family. It's so strong it could pull this tree up by the roots, if it wanted to. Come on now, we'll push ahead, because here, in this spot, I can feel the clenched teeth of all my people in me. I'm finding it hard to breathe.

BEGGAR WOMAN. (*Whines.*) Yiy – yi-yi –

FIRST YOUTH. What's that?

BRIDEGROOM. Go that way. Circle back.

FIRST YOUTH. We're hunting, aren't we? This is a hunt.

BRIDEGROOM. No hunt like it in the world.

(*The* YOUTH *leaves.* BRIDEGROOM *searches, stumbles over the* BEGGAR WOMAN, *Death.*)

BEGGAR WOMAN. (*Whines.*) Yi – yi – i – i!

BRIDEGROOM. What's wrong with you?

BEGGAR WOMAN. I'm cold.

BRIDEGROOM. Where are you going?

BEGGAR WOMAN. Over there, far away...

BRIDEGROOM. Where do you come from?

BEGGAR WOMAN. There, far away...

BRIDEGROOM. Did you see a man and a woman on a galloping horse?

BEGGAR WOMAN. (*Suddenly sharp.*) Give me a moment... (*She looks at him.*) A fine-looking man. Such a handsome, fine-looking man. (*She rises.*) But you'd be even finer-looking if you were asleep. Young and handsome – sleeping.

BRIDEGROOM. Answer me. Did you see a man and a woman on a galloping horse?

BEGGAR WOMAN. Give me a moment.
What strong shoulders you have!
What a strong, firm back!
How would you like to be laid out
On the broad of that back

And never again
Torment your feet with walking,
Your feet, so beautiful and small?
A strong man with small feet – a dream.

BRIDEGROOM. (*Shakes her.*) Did you see them? Answer me! Did they pass this way?

BEGGAR WOMAN. (*Vigorously.*) No, they didn't pass this way. But they're galloping from the hill. Listen! Can you hear them?

BRIDEGROOM. No.

BEGGAR WOMAN. Do you know the road from the hill?

BRIDEGROOM. I'll take it, no matter how rough it is.

BEGGAR WOMAN. I'll go with you. I know this place.

BRIDEGROOM. (*Impatiently.*) All right! Which way?

BEGGAR WOMAN. (*Strongly.*) This way!

(*They leave quickly. Two violins, forest-voices, are heard in the distance.* WOODCUTTERS *return, carrying axes on their shoulders, moving slowly among the trees.*)

FIRST WOODCUTTER. Death! Busy death!
Death touches the leaves!

SECOND WOODCUTTER. Don't release the gushing blood!

FIRST WOODCUTTER. Death! Lonely death!
Death glides through the dry leaves!

THIRD WOODCUTTER. Don't scatter flowers over the wedding!

SECOND WOODCUTTER. Death! Miserable death!
Leave one green branch as a token of their love.

(*They leave as they're talking.*)

(*Enter* LEONARDO *and the* BRIDE.)

LEONARDO. Be still!

BRIDE. Alone, I'll go alone from here.
You must turn back now. Turn back.

LEONARDO. Be quiet!

BRIDE. With your teeth,
        With your hands,
        With anything your blood can imagine,
        Take this chain
        From my clean throat
        And leave me, leave me
        Forgotten
        In my house stuck in the ground.
        If you don't want to kill me
        As you'd kill a little viper
        Put the barrel of your gun
        In my hands, in my hands.
        O what fire of grief and pain
        Roars and sweeps through my head.
        What fierce splinters of glass
        Stick in the roots of my tongue!

LEONARDO. There's no going back. Be quiet!
        They're almost on top of us.
        I'll take you with me!

BRIDE. You'll have to force me then!

LEONARDO. Force? Who was first
        To go down the stairs?

BRIDE. I was.

LEONARDO. Who put the bridle on the horse?

BRIDE. I did.

LEONARDO. Whose hands
        Strapped spurs to my boots?

BRIDE. These hands. And these hands are yours
        And when they see you
        They want to break the blue branches
        And silence forever the voices in your blood.
        I love you! I love you! I love you!
        Leave me!
        If I could kill you
        I'd wrap your body in a shroud
        With violets bordering its edges.
        Violets for love silent and dead!
        What fire of grief and pain
        Roars and sweeps up through my head!

LEONARDO. What fierce splinters of glass
         Stick in the roots of my tongue.
         I tried to forget you,
         Banish you from my heart and mind.
         I built a tall stone wall
         Between your house and mine.
         That's the truth! Do you remember?
         When I saw you in the distance
         I blinded my eyes with sand
         But I was a man on horseback
         And the horse galloped straight to your door.
         And I stood at your wedding
         And the silver pins that you wore
         Made my red blood turn black.
         And the dream of you and me in my body
         Was choking my flesh
         With poisoned weeds.
         It's not my fault,
         Not the fault of my body,
         It's the fault of the earth itself
         And this sweetness that pours from your flesh,
         From your breasts and your hair.

BRIDE. That's not true!
         I want nothing from you,
         Neither table nor bed,
         Yet every minute of every day
         I long to be with you.
         You drag me; I come.
         You tell me to go back,
         I follow you
         Like a leaf blown in the wind.
         I left an honest man, a good man,
         And his people,
         Half-way through the wedding-feast
         Still wearing my crown of flowers.
         But you're the one who will be punished.
         I don't want that to happen.
         Leave me! Go! Get out of here!
         You're all alone!
         There's no one to protect you!

68

LEONARDO. The birds of early morning
Are singing in the trees.
The night is dying
On the stoney ridge.
Come on! We'll go to a quiet place
And I will love you there forever.
I don't care about the people,
I don't care about the poison they fling at us
Out of their sad little hearts.
We two will love. And leave them to their poison.

(*He kisses her passionately.*)

BRIDE. And I'll fall asleep at your feet
And be the guardian of your dreams.
And I'll be naked for you
Letting my eyes wander all over you
Like a bitch in heat
Because that's what I am!
I look at you
And I want you in me,
My one and only man,
In me, your body, deep inside, your body,
Inseparable from mine,
One
Like the unquenchable sun!

LEONARDO. Fire should live with fire,
Flame with burning flame.
Let's go!

BRIDE. Where?

LEONARDO. Where they cannot find us!
Where I can look at you!
Where love can have its way
Free from the poisoned eyes of men and women!

BRIDE. (*With sarcasm.*) Carry me from town to town.
Show me to nice, respectable women.
Let the people see me
With my wedding-sheets
Flapping like banners in the breeze.
Now isn't that a pretty sight?

LEONARDO. If I thought as other men think
I'd want to leave you too!
But listen to the truth!
Where you go, I go.
Where I go, you go.
Try to take a single step away from me.
Try!
Nails of moonlight bind us together,
Your body, my body,
Your bones, my bones.

(*A strong, violent sensuality pervades this entire scene.*)

BRIDE. Listen.

LEONARDO. They're coming.

BRIDE. Run!
I'll die here. That's right and fitting.
Water will cover my feet,
Thorns will stick in my head.
Right and fitting –
The leaves will grieve for me,
Woman lost, virgin gone astray.

LEONARDO. Be quiet. They're here!

BRIDE. Run! Run!

LEONARDO. Quiet! Quiet! We must go! You first!
Now! Don't let them hear us! Go!

(*The* BRIDE *hesitates.*)

BRIDE. Together! One!

LEONARDO. (*Embracing her.*) As you will!
The only way they'll separate us
Is by killing me!

BRIDE. I'll be dead too!

(*They leave, in each other's arms. Stage assumes a strong blue light. The two violins can be heard. Suddenly there are two terrible screams, the violin music is cut short. At the second scream, the* BEGGAR WOMAN *appears, her back to the audience. She opens her cape and stands centre-stage like a huge bird with great wings. The* MOON *halts.*)

[CURTAIN COMES DOWN IN SILENCE]

LAST SCENE

White house, arches, thick walls. Right and left, white stairs. Back, great arch, wall of same colour. Floor is shining white. The house has the feeling of a church. No grey, no shadows whatsoever. Total lucidity.

(TWO GIRLS *in dark blue are winding a red skein.*)

FIRST GIRL. Wool, red wool,
        What shall I make of you?

SECOND GIRL. Dresses of jasmine,
        Wool fine as glass,
        Love in the bridal bed.
        Born at four o'clock,
        By ten o'clock dead.
        One woollen thread
        Will bind your feet down,
        A chain that will fetter
        The bitter white crown.

LITTLE GIRL. (*Sings.*) And were you at the wedding?

FIRST GIRL. No.

LITTLE GIRL. Neither was I!
        Tell me who in the vineyards
        Was chosen to die?
        Tell me who under the olives
        Saw blood running free?
        Tell me who in this world
        Will give love to me?
        And were you at the wedding?

SECOND GIRL. No.

LITTLE GIRL. (*Leaving.*) Neither was I.

SECOND GIRL. Wool, red wool, gentle and strong,
        What is your song?

FIRST GIRL. Their wounds are like wax,
        All terror and fright,
        Sluggish at morning,
        Knife-sharp at night.

LITTLE GIRL. (*At doorway.*)
  This red thread staggers
  Over the stones,
  Over mountains, blue mountains,
  Dead lovers' bones.
  See the red thread run,
  Run, run, run,
  Red thread, red thread, red thread,
  Stick in the knife,
  Take out the bread.

(*She leaves.*)

SECOND GIRL. Wool, red wool. Tender and strong,
  What is your song?

FIRST GIRL. Lovers together
  All blood and gore;
  I saw their bodies
  Stretched out on the shore.

(*She stops, looks at the skein of red wool.*)

LITTLE GIRL. (*At doorway.*)
  The red thread is running,
  Running, running, running,
  Wild love galloped away,
  Dead love returning;
  On the road the sunlight greets
  Bodies wrapped in ivory sheets.

(*Leonardo's* WIFE *and* MOTHER-IN-LAW *appear, in great distress.*)

FIRST GIRL. Are they coming this way?

MOTHER-IN-LAW. (*Harshly.*) I don't know.

SECOND GIRL. Tell us about the wedding!

FIRST GIRL. Yes, tell us, tell us!

MOTHER-IN-LAW. (*Curtly.*) Nothing to tell.

WIFE. I want to go back, find out everything.

MOTHER-IN-LAW. (*Sternly.*) Go back to your house,
  Stay there, brave and alone.
  Cry your tears and grow old
  Behind closed doors.

No more. Never again, dead or alive.
We'll blot out the daylight,
Nail up the windows
Where the cold heart bleeds
And the black rain batters
The bitter weeds.

WIFE. What happened?

MOTHER-IN-LAW. What happened?
It doesn't matter what happened!
Cover your face with a veil!
Your children belong to you.
That's all!
Live with your loss!
On the bed
Where his pillow was
Place a cross of ashes.

(*They leave.*)

BEGGAR WOMAN. (*At door.*)
Dear girls, kind girls,
A crumb of bread, a crust of bread.

LITTLE GIRL. Go away! Get out of here!

(*The* GIRLS *huddle together.*)

BEGGAR WOMAN. Why?

LITTLE GIRL. Because you whine and cringe and beg.
Go away! Go away!

FIRST GIRL. Child!

BEGGAR WOMAN. I could have begged for your eyes!
A cloud of birds is following me!
Would you like to pick
A bird out of the cloud?

LITTLE GIRL. I want to go away from here!

SECOND GIRL. (*To the* BEGGAR WOMAN.)
O never mind her!

FIRST GIRL. How did you come?
By the road near the stream?

BEGGAR WOMAN. Yes.

FIRST GIRL. (*Timidly*.) Can you tell me something?

BEGGAR WOMAN. I saw them.
They'll be here in a little while:
Two torrents
Peaceful at last,
Among the huge rocks,
Two men at the horse's feet,
Two dead men
In the calm, beautiful night.

(*With great pleasure.*)

Dead. Dead.

FIRST GIRL. Be quiet, old woman, be quiet.

BEGGAR WOMAN. Instead of eyes – crushed flowers!
Instead of teeth – spikes of frozen snow!
Two men died, the bride returns alive,
Their blood staining her clothes and hair.
Two dead men wrapped in sheets
On the shoulders of powerful boys!
That's the story! That's all! No more!
Something passes
Over the dirty sand and the golden flower!

(*She leaves.* THE GIRLS *bow their heads, start to leave in rhythm.*)

FIRST GIRL. Dirty sand.

SECOND GIRL. Golden flower.

LITTLE GIRL. Over the golden flower
They're bringing the dead
Along the road by the stream,
Two dark men,
Two dark men.
A dark nightingale flashes and cries
Over the golden flower!
Work is a long life. Love is a short hour.

(*She leaves. Empty stage.* MOTHER *and* NEIGHBOUR WOMAN *come on. The* NEIGHBOUR *is crying.*)

MOTHER. Sh-ssh.

NEIGHBOUR. I can't.

MOTHER. Be quiet.
(*At the door.*)
Is there anybody there?

(*She covers her face with her hands.*)

My son should be answering me. But my son is withered flowers turning to dust. My son is fading into nothing beyond the mountains.

(*In rage, to the* NEIGHBOUR.)

Will you shut up? Stop whining and crying! I want no crying in this house! Your tears come easily from your eyes, but when I'm alone my tears will pour from my bones, my veins, my heart, and they will hurt more than my burning blood!

NEIGHBOUR. Come with me, to my house. You mustn't stay here.

MOTHER. I'll stay here. Here is where I want to be. Nowhere else. Here. In peace. They're all dead. And I'll find peace at midnight in my sleep, sleep without the fear of knives and guns. Let other women stand at their windows, searching the rain for their sons' faces. I will not. I'll dream in peace unknown to men; and of my dreams I'll make a cold ivory dove to carry frosty camellias to the graves of my loved ones. Graves! No, no, not graves – sweet beds of earth that shelter them, cradles that rock them to peaceful sleep in the sky! God in heaven, leave me my dream of peace!

(*Enter a* WOMAN IN BLACK, *goes right, kneels.*)

(*To the* NEIGHBOUR.) Take your hands from your face. We have bad days ahead. I don't want to see anybody. There's the earth. There's me. There's my grief. And these four walls. Aah! (*She sits down, spent.*)

NEIGHBOUR. Go easy on yourself!

MOTHER. (*Pushing back her hair.*) I must try to be calm. Calm – because my neighbours, all the women, will come and see me; and I don't want to let them see me so weak and poor. Poor! So poor! A woman without even a single son that she can hold close against her lips!

(*The* BRIDE *appears, without her wreath, wearing a black shawl.*)

NEIGHBOUR. (*In rage, seeing* BRIDE.) Where's d'you think you're going?

BRIDE. I'm here.

MOTHER. (*To* NEIGHBOUR.) Who's that?

NEIGHBOUR. Don't you know her?

MOTHER. That's why I asked you who she is. I *mustn't* know her, I *cannot* know her, because if I do I'll sink my teeth into her throat. Viper!

(*She moves in rage towards the* BRIDE, *stops.*)

(*To the* NEIGHBOUR.) Look at her! Standing there, crying. And look at me, standing here, and I'm not tearing her eyes out! What's this? What's wrong? I can't understand myself. My son – did I love my son? Where is his good name? Where is my son's good name? His good name? Where is it? Where is it?

(*She beats the* BRIDE *who falls to floor.*)

NEIGHBOUR. Stop, stop it, for God's sake!

BRIDE. Don't stop her! Let her kill me! I came here so she'd kill me and then they'd have to take me away with the dead.

(*To the* MOTHER.) But don't kill me with your hands! Kill me with hooks and knives and scythes – kill me with all the strength of your body and soul – use knives and scythes and hooks to cut and hack my flesh into my bones! Kill me – so I'll know I'll be clean! I want you to know I'm clean, although I may be mad. And I want you to see them bury me, knowing that not a single man has lain upon the whiteness of my breasts.

MOTHER. Shut up! What do I care about all that?

BRIDE. I ran away with another man! I ran away!

(*With anguish.*) You'd have gone too! I was a woman crazed with passionate desire, festering inside and out, all sores, and your son was like cool, good water to give me children, land, health; but the other man was a dark, deep river, full of leaves and twigs and branches, that brought me a hidden music and a whispered song. And I walked by your son's side. He was like a boy made of cool, good water; and the other man sent towards me packed and clamouring flocks of birds that blocked my way and left white frost on my wounds, the wounds of a withered woman, the wounds of a girl caressed by subtle fingers of fire. I didn't want to do what I did! Remember that! I didn't want to! Your son was the right and only man for me, and I have not betrayed your son, but the other man dragged me along like a tidal wave, like a butt from a mule's head, dragging me, pulling me, sweeping me away, always, always, always – even if I were a withered old hag and every one of your son's sons were pulling me back and holding me down by the hair.

(*A* NEIGHBOUR *enters*.)

MOTHER. She's not to blame. Neither am I!
(*Sarcastically*.) Well, who's to blame, then? A sleepless, restless, lazy, delicate woman who throws away a crown of orange-blossoms and goes off looking for a bed warmed by another woman!

BRIDE. That's enough! I'm here! Take your revenge! Look! Look! My throat is soft – you'd have less trouble cutting my throat than a flower in your garden. But no, not that! Never that! Clean, clean as a newborn child! I'm pure! And strong enough to prove it to you! Light the fire! We'll stick our hands in the fire! You, for your son. Me, for my body. You'll be the first to pull your hands out of the fire!

(*Enter another* NEIGHBOUR.)

MOTHER. Purity! Fire! What does your good name matter to me? And what does your death matter to me? What does any single thing about your body and mind and soul matter to me? My sons are buried under the wheat – blessed be the wheat. The rain soaks like a kiss into the dust of my buried sons – blessed be the rain. And God, in His own good time, will stretch us all out together, to rest – blessed be God.

(*Enter another* NEIGHBOUR.)

BRIDE. Let me join you in grief. Let me weep at your side.

MOTHER. Weep – but at the door.

(*The* LITTLE GIRL *enters. The* BRIDE *stays at door. The* MOTHER *is at centre-stage*.)

WIFE. (*Enters, goes left.*)
> He was a prince of horsemen,
> Now he's a heap of snow.
> To towns and fairs and mountains,
> Into women's arms –
> That's where he loved to go.
> Now, the dark, damp moss of night
> Lies on his forehead.

MOTHER. A sunflower for your mother,
> Perfect mirror of the earth.
> Let a cross of bitter rosebay
> Be placed upon your breast.
> Let a sheet of whitest silk
> Cover you tonight
> And between your quiet hands
> Let water make its cry.

WIFE. Ah! Four young men,
> Their shoulders sore
> From carrying the dead!

BRIDE. Ah! Four young men!
> They've carried death on high
> For miles and miles!

MOTHER. Neighbours.

LITTLE GIRL. (*At door.*)
> They're bringing them in.

MOTHER. In the end, always the same thing.
> The Cross. The Cross.

WOMEN. Nails. Cross.
> The sweetest name ever heard.
> Jesus Christ, our Lord.

BRIDE. May the Cross protect
> The living and the dead.

MOTHER. Neighbours:
> With a knife, with a small knife,
> On a day that had to happen,
> Between two and three o'clock,
> These two men killed each other for love.

With a knife,
A small knife,
So small it barely fits the hand
Yet slips in clean
Through the disbelieving flesh
And sticks
In the very roots of pain.

BRIDE. And here is a knife
A small knife
So small it barely fits the hand,
So small but, heart of Christ, so deadly:
On a day that had to happen
Between two and three o'clock,
With this knife,
Two men are dead,
Their bodies gone to dust,
All with a small knife.

MOTHER. So small,
It barely fits the hand
But slips in clean
Through the disbelieving flesh
And sticks
In the very roots of pain
Where death is born
And love dies
And I am left
With the torn, dirty remnants of a dream,
A dream that I must change,
In this blood-haunted place,
Into a dream of peace.

[CURTAIN]

FEDERICO GARCÍA LORCA

Selected Poems

Bilingual Spanish-English edition translated by
MERRYN WILLIAMS

'I realised I had been murdered.
They searched cafés, cemeteries, churches.
They opened barrels and cupboards.
And plundered three skeletons
for their gold teeth.
But they never found me?
No. They never found me.'

Federico García Lorca, Spain's greatest modern poet and dramatist, was murdered by Fascist partisans in 1936, shortly after the outbreak of the Spanish Civil War. He was by then an immensely popular figure, celebrated throughout the Spanish-speaking world, and at the height of his creative powers. After his death, with his work suppressed, he became a potent symbol of the martyrdom of Spain.

The manuscript of Lorca's last poems, his tormented *Sonnets of Dark Love*, disappeared during the Civil War. For fifty years the poems lived only in the words of the poets who had heard Lorca read them, like Neruda and Aleixandre, who remembered them as 'a pure and ardent monument to love in which the prime material is now the poet's flesh, his heart, his soul wide open to his own destruction'. Lorca's lost sonnets were recently re-discovered in Spain, and this is the first book to include English translations of these brooding poems.

Merryn Williams' new edition draws on the full range of Lorca's poetry, from the early poems and the gypsy ballads to the agitated *Poet in New York* sequence and the Arab-influenced gacelas and casidas which followed his American exile. It includes the *Lament for Ignacio Sánchez Mejías*, Lorca's great elegy for his bullfighter friend, as well as the full text of his famous lecture on the *duende*, the daemon of Spanish music, song, dance, poetry and art.

In these remarkable translations, Lorca's elemental poems are reborn in English, with their stark images of blood and moon, of water and earth; of bulls, horses and fish; olives, sun and oranges; knives and snow; darkness and death.